IF I DO SAY SO MYSELF

More Thoughts About Faith and Life

Richard Stoll Armstrong

Illustrations by
Bil Canfield

Richard S. Armstrong
Publisher

IF I DO SAY SO MYSELF

First Edition
Copyright © 1997 by
Richard S. Armstrong

Scripture quotations, unless marked otherwise, are from the *Revised Standard Version of the Bible*, copyrighted 1946, 1952 (c), 1971, 1973, by the Division of Christian Education of the National Council of the Churches of Christ in the USA. Used by permission.

Scripture quotations marked (NRSV) are from the *New Revised Standard Version of the Bible*, copyright 1989 by the Division of Christian Education of the National Council of the Churches of Christ in the USA. Used by permission.

Scripture quotations marked (NIV) are from the *HOLY BIBLE, NEW INTERNATIONAL VERSION*. Copyright (c) 1973, 1978, 1984 International Bible Society. Used by permission of Zondervan Bible Publishers. All rights reserved.

Library of Congress Catalog Card Number: 96-94892

ISBN 0-7880-0918-4   PRINTED IN U.S.A.

CONTENTS

Preface

This collection of poetry, which covers a wide variety of topics, has been divided into three sections. Some of the poems were inspired by my devotional reading of the Bible, although they are usually "take-offs" on the text, rather than expositions of it. I have grouped these in the first section under the heading "From Biblical Texts." The corresponding scripture passages are listed in the endnotes.

In the second section, subtitled "Random Thoughts," are poems which were triggered by some of my own experiences and observations of life. There is no unifying theme.

If I Do Say So Myself has been even longer in the making than my previous volumes, as these poems cover a span of more than fifty years. The earliest was written during my sophomore year at Princeton, long before I ever dreamed of becoming a minister. It is included with two other poems in the third section under the heading "From My Distant Past."

Many of the poems in the first two sections were written to be used in a sermon or talk, while for others I had no particular use in mind. In every case they represent an attempt to express poetically my thoughts regarding some aspect of faith or life, sometimes humorously, more often seriously.

As I have explained in the prefaces of my two previous poetry books, *Enough, Already!* (Fairway Press, 1993) and *Now, That's a Miracle!* (CSS, 1996), my poems are written to be read aloud, as well as silently. In addition to their being used in personal devotions and meditation, I hope they will also be a helpful source of illustrations for pastors, teachers, and others in their preaching and speaking. To that end, I have included a topical index and an index of first lines. CSS is happy to allow churches to print all or parts of a poem in their worship bulletins and newsletters, with proper credits, of course.

It has been a pleasure to work again with my favorite illustrator, Bil Canfield, whose drawings enhance the impact of the poems and enliven the entire book. He has a remarkable gift of being able to portray so simply and effectively the ideas that I try to communicate to him with my rough sketches and verbal descriptions. Bil is a most versatile artist, whose sensitivity is reflected in his drawings. I am deeply indebted to Bil for his amazing productivity, total dependability, and ungrudging flexibility. He is a valued colleague and a cherished friend.

Finally, I want to express, as I always do, my undying gratitude to my wonderful wife Margie. She has been my most trusted and reliable critic, without whose patience, forbearance, and encouragement I would never take the time to indulge my poetic proclivities.

Princeton, New Jersey   R.S.A.

Dedicated
with a father's
gratitude,
love, and pride
to
Ellen, Ricky,
Andy, Woody,
and Elsie

Section One:

FROM BIBLICAL TEXTS

IF I DO SAY SO MYSELF[1]

One word about humility,

    which surely won't exhaust it:

The moment that you say you have it,

    you've already lost it!

ROOM FOR MORE[2]

(A Brief Commentary on the Doctrine of Election)

Many are called,

    but few are chosen.

That doesn't mean

    the number's frozen.

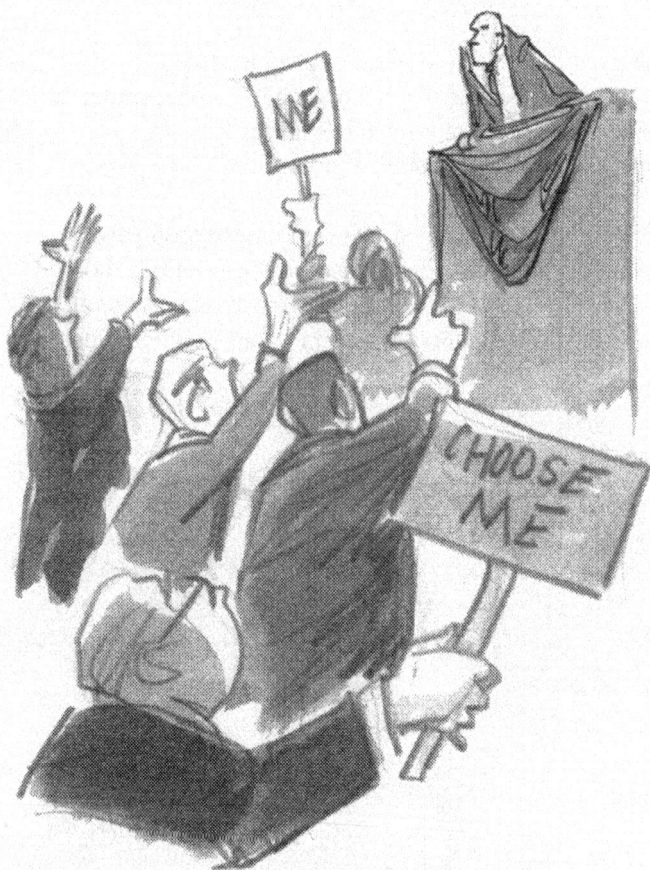

FOUL WEATHER FRIENDS[3]

When the sky is bright blue with clear sailing ahead.
　　when your worries are few and your troubles have fled,
you can bet that you'll find you're surrounded with friends,
　　as if on your favor their future depends.

When your pockets are full and the world's at your feet,
　　you will get invitations to join the elite,
for it's not too hard then for some folks to be nice.
　　They will wine you and dine you and seek your advice.

But the question to ask yourself once in a while,
　　when you're getting a slap on the back with a smile,
is, What will become of your fair weather friends,
　　when the going gets rough and your influence ends?

Can you count on them then, when you need their support,
　　when your luck has run out and your efforts fall short?
That's the test! And the best are the foul weather friends
　　who are still by your side when the fair weather ends!

MISSING THE MOMENT[4]

Living for some future day?

Always wishing time away?

To miss the moment of today

is such a costly price to pay!

GETTING READY FOR CHRISTMAS[5]

Working, slaving, pennies saving,
shopping, waiting, long lines hating,
sewing, pressing, cards addressing,
buying, trying, washing, drying,
licking, sticking, presents picking,
making, baking, early waking,
capping, wrapping, never napping,
lighting, writing, stopping fighting,
messing, meaning vacuum cleaning,
memory versing, parts rehearsing,
car pool driving, late arriving,
parties throwing, money's going,
sick kids nursing, feel like cursing,
surely this must not be Christmas!

BLACK AND WHITE[6]

How can anyone blame a black person today
  for not taking us whites at our word?
When what we are doing is not what we say,
  do we have any right to be heard?

It was there all the time but we whites couldn't hear
  the resentment and pain of the blacks.
Was it apathy, ignorance, hatred, or fear
  that made so many whites turn their backs?

We have talked to the point where mere talk is a sin.
  All our rhetoric falls on deaf ears.
Blacks are waiting to see when we whites will begin
  what we should have been doing for years.

What amazes me more than our white sinfulness,
  which is proof of humanity's Fall,
is the fact that despite all we have to confess,
  our black neighbors can trust us at all!

"WE'RE NUMBER ONE!"[7]

To be a good loser is challenge enough.
    To be a good winner is equally tough!
Few things ever gall me more under the sun
    than hearing some braggarts shout "We're Number One!"
I have to declare that it sure gets my goat,
    when even the teams that I'm rooting for gloat.
For boxers or merchants or teams and their fans,
    for leaders of nations and vain "also-rans,"
For armies and navies and their personnel,
    for whoever wins and their boosters as well,
it ill behooves any to flaunt their success.
    Sincere gratitude is what they should express.
I think when those characters seem so cock sure,
    too bad they don't know what "pride goeth before"!

JUST KIDDING![8]

If you want folks
to like your jokes,
yourself of friends not ridding,
it doesn't pay
to sting, and say
"But I am only kidding!"

Time and again
some rascals when
their hurtful fun are poking,
employ that ruse!
It's no excuse
to say, "I'm only joking!"

THE WEARER OF THIS BADGE HAS FAITH[9]

Christian faith is a strange paradox,

I would say,

in that faith never shows when it's put

on display.

THE HALF-SHEKEL TAX[10]

Some collectors asked Peter the facts:
"Does your Christ pay the half-shekel tax?"
Peter took a good guess
and his answer was, "Yes!"
Jesus said to him later, "Relax!"

Then he told Peter, "Go cast a hook.
Take the first fish you catch, and then look
in its mouth you will find
one whole shekel. Be kind
to pay your tax and mine by the book."

With an eye to the main chance then Peter
deduced, "What could ever be neater?
I'll obey Jesus' wish
and cut open the fish.
If I don't find a coin, I can eat her."

TALKERS AND DOERS[11]

So shy are some about their faith
    they wouldn't lead in silent prayer.
But when it's time to take a stand
    for Jesus Christ, you find them there.
Contrast them with those vocal saints,
    who act as if they're heaven sent.
But when the hard choice must be made,
    you wonder where those talkers went!

THE RIGHT TO BE HEARD[12]

Ordination confers upon preachers the right

    to proclaim from the pulpit God's Word.

Though they may have been given the right to proclaim,

    they must merit the right to be heard.

STORAGE POLICY[13]

We have a safe deposit box
    to keep our treasures in.
I've never thought that prudent step
    was any kind of sin.
Our house had been twice burglarized.
    A third attempt was foiled.
We lost heirlooms, and wedding gifts,
    and things for which we'd toiled.
But then I thought of Jesus' words
    about treasures on earth,
where moths consume and thieves break in.
    How much are those things worth?
He said to lay up treasures in
    the heavens up above.
I think he meant the lasting things,
    like faith, and hope, and love.
So storage vaults and bank accounts
    we don't have to condemn,
as long as we don't value life
    by what we have in them.

LET THE ABUSERS COME, TOO[14]

With incidents of child abuse
    becoming so widespread,
the world needs to confess its sin
    and heed what Jesus said
about preventing little ones
    from coming to the Son,
whose kingdom they belong to and
    who cherishes each one.
How much abuse could soon be stopped,
    if people only knew
that Jesus yearns to heal and save
    the child abusers, too!

TRUE FRIENDS[15]

True friends do not discourage me from doing what I must.
True friends are those whose knowledge of my duty I can trust.
True friends don't make it difficult to do the thing I should.
True friends support me in my quest for what is true and good.
True friends don't try to keep me from the higher harder ways.
True friends are those I need and want to be my friends always.

SAYERS AND DOERS[16]

When it comes to friends it seems there are two types.
You can't always separate them by their stripes.
While both call themselves your friends,
are they really? That depends,
for with some I bet you've had your share of gripes.

I refer to those who tell you what they'll do,
but who never do the things they promise to.
Can you call someone a friend
on whose word you can't depend,
and when help is needed never does come through?

There are those who say they won't but then they do it.
There are those who say they will but don't get to it.
When it comes to things that matter,
don't be hoodwinked by the latter.
If you count on what they say they'll do, you'll rue it!

THE POLLUTED PLANET[17]

Isaiah's words of long ago are relevant today,
    prophetic to an ominous degree:
Polluted lies the planet Earth, as its inhabitants
    are poisoning the air, the land, the sea.

The toxic wastes, the urban blight, the suffocating smog,
    are symptoms and the causes of disease.
for human beings choke beneath pollution's brownish pall,
    which also threatens birds and beasts and trees.

God gave humanity dominion over all the world,
    which God created beautiful and good.
But we have squandered and misused the riches of the earth,
    instead of being stewards, as we should.

The ruthlessness of power and the arrogance of wealth
    have dulled the human heart to human need.
So millions live in poverty and die from lack of food,
    the victims of our apathy and greed.

God's statutes have been broken and God's laws have been
transgressed,
    and surely we shall suffer for our sin.
The madness of a race to arms of nuclear design
    was leading to a war no one could win.

What senseless folly drives us down this self-destructive course?
    How can we dare ignore our sacred trust
from God, to tend the universe and care for all of life?
    By God's grace that we can do —and we must!

THE BEST LAID PLANS. . .[18]

Woe to those whose best laid plans
    do not include the Lord,
whose military strategy
    meets not with God's accord.
Woe to all the nations when
    their treaties go awry,
for trusting in alliances
    instead of the Most High.
Woe to those who stockpile arms
    but don't give prayer a nod,
and yet they proudly claim to be
    one nation under God!

THE GOSPEL IN A WORD[19]

"Tell us the gospel in one word,
if you would like to please us."
"The gospel in one word you ask?
The good news word is 'Jesus'!
All aspects of the gospel have
to do with God's Son Jesus.
To know him is to know the one
who loves, forgives, and frees us.
He is the good news in one word,
our one true Lord and Savior.
If we believe the good news, it
should show in our behavior!"

IN DEFENSE OF NIGHT PERSONS[20]

We put in just as long a day as early risers do.

    The hours that we spend in bed are relatively few.

If early in the morning we are not a perky pup,

    it's just because we go to bed when some are getting up!

RISE-AND-SHINERS[21]

Hats off to those persons who rise before dawn
    to study the scriptures and pray.
They're doing what Jesus did long, long ago,
    while I'm in bed snoring away.

In fact, they are doing much better than Christ,
    for where, may I ask, does it say
in Matthew or Mark, or in Luke, or in John,
    that Jesus did that every day?

OFFENSE OR OFFENSIVENESS?[22]

When the gospel is presented it can easily offend.

But remember it's the gospel, not the witnesses' chief end!

The offense that people speak of in the gospel we proclaim

is no call to be offensive, when we speak in Jesus' name.

SOMETHING YOU FIND YOURSELF WITH[23]

That one can believe what one cannot conceive

is somewhat akin to a myth.

For faith is not something you make yourself have;

it's something you find yourself with.

COULD GOD FORGET?[24]

Thus says the Lord to one abhorred, whom all despise:
"Kings shall arise, and they shall all before you fall
because of me, as you will see. For I have heard your pleading
word and will this day help you to say to those in chains, where
darkness reigns, 'Come forth!' They'll feed, and every need will
be supplied. I'll be their guide by mountain springs. The whole
earth sings, and heaven, too, will sing anew! For I the Lord have
thus assured my people of my steadfast love."

But Zion said, "It seems instead not so. Has he forsaken me?"

The Lord replied to cheer and chide: "Could I forget? How
could I let you go? Your wall and gates so tall before me stand.
And on my hand I've graven you. Your builders do what those
who would destroy you could prevent not. They were chased away.
And as I live, my word I give. Your enemy your slave will be —
an ornament that's heaven sent, and by you worn as would adorn a
bride. I'll do this, and to you that promise make, for my name's
sake!"

NO MOA!²⁵

When there came to the Ark a big moa,
to that moa old Noah said "Whoa!
We will take the emu,
but there's no room for you!"
And that's why the moa's no moa!

WHO LET HER IN?[26]

There once was a woman of sin,
who forgiveness from Jesus did win.
For his feet she did douse
in a Pharisee's house.
Now, my question is, Who let her in?

KNOW YOUR ENEMIES[27]

One thing about church members that
    has always bothered me
is, some of them don't seem to know
    who is the enemy!
They criticize their pastors, who
    are striving to do good,
instead of working with them to
    change sinners, as they should.

TOO QUICK TO SCOLD[28]

Impatiently and hastily
in manner far from mild
too often I have scolded or
rebuked my little child,
and then discovered later on,
much to my deep chagrin,
that I was wrong and he was right.
My anger was the sin!
If we would only listen first,
how often we would find
the little tykes we're quick to blame
have something good in mind.

FINGER POINTING[29]

I think that I would be much less
    inclined to criticize,
if I could just be guided by
    this little exercise.

I learned it when I was a child.
    It's just as true today.
I need to do it now and then
    to govern what I say.

I point my finger at someone
    and I at once can see:
one finger points to him or her,
    three fingers point to me!

PEER PRESSURE[30]

To be considered "different" is for some kids pretty rough.

And so they often end up being not different enough!

They're far too influenced by what their peers may say or think,

and so they feel they can't say no to drugs, or sex, or drink.

DISAGREEING CHRISTIANS[31]

Some Christians eat meat on Friday; other Christians don't.

Some Christians will have a cocktail; other Christians won't.

Some have been baptized by sprinkling; some have been immersed.

Some say they don't know the Bible; others are well-versed.

Not all Christians in communion use a common cup.

Some are sitting, some are kneeling, some are standing up.

Some just bow their heads when praying; others kneel to pray.

Some think standing with their hands raised is the Spirit's way.

Some think that the King James Version is THE Holy Book;

translations that others favor rate no second look.

Some don't use the creeds in worship; some do all the time.

Some Christians are more than tithers; some don't give a dime.

Some stick closely to tradition; others innovate.

Some do not like "modern" music; others think it's great.

Some Christians won't speak at meetings; others use their voice.

Some argue against abortion; others are pro-choice.

Some think one should not remarry, having been divorced;

others think Jesus' restriction should not be enforced.

These are but a few examples. You don't have to search

to find points of disagreement in the Christian Church.

But the most important issue in the push and shove,

is: Should Christians not know how to disagree in love?

VINDICATION[32]

People often do things to us that are mean, unfair, and wrong,
    and we never get the pleasure of revenge.
So we go through life unvindicated, nursing all along
    our resentment for the wrongs we can't avenge.

We've been overcharged and cheated and unjustly criticized,
    and have failed to get the credit we deserve;
our ideas have been stolen and our houses burglarized,
    and we've often been deceived or thrown a curve.

If we only could remember and then really take to heart
    what it means to say that vengeance is the Lord's.
When we trust God's vindication and don't seek it on our part,
    what amazing peace of mind our faith affords!

We shall have our vindication, but it will not be the way
    a vindictive person oft' retaliates,
for revenge is not our proper aim, and we do not repay.
    It is God who justifies and vindicates.

It is only through the eyes of faith that we can understand
    when and how we're vindicated by the Lord.
I confess, though, even when things work out better than I'd
planned
    I'm still nursing the resentment I have stored.

I am being very sinful, when I feel this way, I know,
    for I'm totally ignoring what God said.
My own faith is fluctuating, as these feelings come and go.
    Only God can take the mean thoughts from my head.

And although I'm truly grateful for the way things work for good,
  I confess I still resent the people who
never seem to get the punishment or blame I think they should.
  I must have my vengeful cake and eat it, too!

Section Two:

RANDOM THOUGHTS

THE VIEWING

As was to be expected,
many came
to Thelma's viewing.
Most were doing
their final duty to the deceased.
One, whose name
is best unmentioned,
was not so well intentioned,
as she had ceased
to be Thelma's friend
long before the end.
She didn't really care
and was there
more out of curiosity
than any virtuosity.
She wondered how
this extravagant eccentric, who
never was concerned about
income tax deductions,
and who once had been her sacred cow,
would be laid out.
For she knew
Thelma had left explicit instructions
regarding her funeral arrangements, and she
was here to see if it would be,
as she suspected,
the most expensive coffin one could find,
the kind
that only Thelma would have bought.
So thought
this former friend.
It was near the end
when she came and stood
by the casket, head bowed,

in ostensible respect
as others in the crowd
would expect
her to. "Doesn't she look good?"
someone whispered in a tone so often
used around the dead.
Thelma's former friend responded with a noncommittal
    smile,
staring all the while
at the flower bedecked coffin
with the stylishly garbed corpse lying serenely in it.
After what seemed at least a minute,
Thelma's former friend turned and headed for the door.
Shaking her head in undisguised disgust,
and in a voice she must
have wanted everyone to hear,
(at least her words were clear
from where I sat)
Thelma's one-time friend said
"I wouldn't be caught dead
in a coffin like that!"

STAY PUT, MR. FOSS!

"Let me live in a house by the side of the road

and be a friend to man."

With all due respect to old Sam Walter Foss,

I don't know how anyone can!

It's not just his language to which I object.

Inclusive or not, it's the thought.

I have a suspicion the poet elect,

if it had been my house that he bought,

would find himself surely agreeing with me,

before a few days had gone by.

For all of the trash that is dumped on our lawn

would make any home owner cry.

From beer cans and bottles to Styrofoam cups,

old clothing and cigarette butts,

scrap metal and garbage and furniture, too,

and even dead cats and dead mutts.

How can I befriend all those mean litterbugs

whizzing by in their cars and their trucks?

Their thoughtless pollution deserves only wrath

—and a fine of a few hundred bucks!

So take my advice and ignore Mr. Foss,

though he was a remarkable man.

If he moved to a house by the side of the road,

he would need a much bigger trash can!

YOU'RE WELCOME, I GUESS

It always used to irk me,
    if when I held a door,
I got no smile or thanks from
    the one I held it for.

To that ungrateful person
    I then would turn and say,
"You're welcome, sir (or madam)"
    in my most pleasant way.

But now I ask myself where
    my altruism ranks,
If when I act politely,
    I do it just for thanks.

DILEMMA OF A WOULD-BE ACTIVIST

I profess to be innocent of the sins of my forbears,
        but am I, really?
I disclaim my complicity in the cause of your plight,
        but can I, really?
I say I hear your angry rhetoric,
        but do I, really?
I wonder why you do not trust my worthy declarations,
        but should I, really?
I claim to identify with you in your struggle,
        but have I, really?
I know there is something I can and must do,
        but will I —really?

A VIOLENT WORLD

The violence surrounding us is frightening to see—

   the child abuse, and spouse abuse, police brutality.

It's on our streets and in our homes, it's on the movie screens.

   It punctuates the language of adults as well as teens.

It fills the daily papers and it dominates the news.

   It saturates the television programs people choose.

It's how some people root for teams, and how they drive a car,

   and how they flaunt the litter laws, no matter where they are.

It's their abuse of others' rights, their treatment of the poor.

   It's what they do in their aggressive grabs for more and more.

It's gross neglect of neighborhoods where poverty abounds,

   it's water, air, and land misuse, offensive sights and sounds.

It's acts of terrorism that do not seem to abate.

   It's ethnic cleansing, racial hatred, bigotry, and hate.

It's what some do to animals and their environment.

   It's corporate crime, the mafia, and sleazy government.

It's slaughtering endangered species 'til they are all gone.

   It's all of this and much, much more —one could go on and on.

As violence breeds violence, we'll pay the price, because

the whole world is the victim when a few transgress God's laws.

How much worse, then, the consequence of violence and strife, when for so many it has now become a way of life.

YES I DO MIND!

When will some smokers ever learn

    it's not polite or kind

to light a pipe or cigarette

    while asking, "Do you mind?"

UNDER THE INFLUENCE

All drunken drivers are a threat
    to others and themselves, and yet,
there's overwhelming evidence
    to show that most car accidents
are caused by social drinkers who
    have had no more than one or two!
Contrary to what some fools think,
    it's dangerous to take a drink
before you get behind the wheel,
    because one drink can make you feel
that you're completely in control.
    but that one drink can take its toll
on your reaction time and make
    you take some risks your shouldn't take,
like speeding through a yellow light,
    or passing someone on the right.
So many people drink these days,
    that they'll not likely change their ways.
There's nothing wrong, most would agree,
    with someone's drinking socially.
The problem isn't what they think;
    the problem is, they drive and drink!

HAPPINESS IS BEING A GRANDPARENT

I never understood
until I, too,
became a grandparent,
and then I knew
that all the good things said
by people who
themselves are grandparents
indeed are true!

WHOSE DEPARTMENT?

As a minister
I'm often told
by my old tennis friends,
with good humor
but half-serious intent,
"Now the weather
is in your department,
Reverend!"
That depends!
I remind them,
I'm in sales
not management!

SMOKING

I sympathize with those who have the habit and can't shake it.
I empathize with those with allergies who cannot take it.
I ostracize the ones whose tainted breath and clothes announce it.
I eulogize the folks who used to smoke and now denounce it.
I criticize those people who despite the risks still do it.
I agonize with those who've lost a friend or loved one to it.
I socialize with those who gave it up or never did it.
I patronize those restaurants and places which forbid it.
I chastise those who jeopardize the health of others by it.
I scrutinize the ads designed to make young people try it.
I minimize permission for those smokers who request it.
I maximize the use of signs, and if none, I suggest it.
I theorize no one would smoke who really understands it.
I sermonize the stewardship of life clearly demands it.

LABELS

"Conservative" and "liberal" are labels I abhor.
    The way they're used today they have no meaning any more.
I hate it when somebody pins a tag like that on me.
    For labels put you in a slot you do not want to be.
Whatever people want to call themselves, they should feel free,
    but not too many folks I know do so consistently
on social issues, politics, religion, war and peace,
    the Bible, life-style, language, drugs —the issues never cease.
One may be quite conservative in some things, not in all.
    To pin that label on someone, then, takes "a lot of gall"!
I wish some self-named liberals would give more liberally.
    I wish some staunch conservatives would live more morally.
More liberal in spirit is what we should strive to be.
    In life-style more conservative, on that can we agree?
So when we use those labels let us be much more select,
    for neither label is a proof that one's of the elect!

BUMPER STICKERS

Bumper stickers advertise
  more than some folks realize.
Of the ones that I have seen
  some are funny, some are mean.
Some are thoughtful, some inane,
  some religious, some profane,
Some suggestive, some obscene,
  some political and mean.
Some are boastful, some inflame,
  some pay tribute, some defame.
Every bumper sticker tells
  more than simply what it sells.
It shows what the values are
  of the owner of the car.

THINGS HAVE CHANGED!

Yesterday's outlawed pornography
   is today's display photography.
      Things have certainly changed!
What they call the new morality
   is just the old immorality.
      Things have certainly changed!
The most bizarre sexuality
   is passed off as liberality.
      Things have certainly changed!
What is the moral authority
   of the immoral majority?
      Things have certainly changed!
Have they weighed the liability
   of their irresponsibility?
      Things have certainly changed!
Why can't people see the gravity
   of their own worldly depravity?
      Things must certainly change!

SLACKERS

Some folks mean to
but don't lean to.
They just dally,
but don't rally;
prone to shirking,
loath to working;
always ruing,
never doing;
alibiing,
but not trying.
They can't take it,
so they fake it.
Don't mistake it,
they won't make it!

JOGGING

When I first started out on my jogging career,
    to a friend I remarked with a smile,
"If I jog every day, by the end of the year
    I'll be able to run a whole mile!"

I decided to start at a pace I could keep,
    so I'd have something left at the end.
I'll admit it was tough, and those slopes seemed so steep—
    how much effort I had to expend!

Not a few of my colleagues thought I was insane,
    and they simply could not comprehend
why a person my age should submit to that pain.
    "But it's worth it," I'd say, "in the end."

For my heart and my lungs were now functioning well,
    and my weight was where it ought to be.
It was great to feel fit, and my friends now could see
    that it sure had done wonders for me.

Later on I decided to enter a race
    just to see how it felt to compete.
I was not too concerned about where I would place;
    just to run was enough of a feat.

That experience taught me a lesson or two
    that I'll carry the rest of my days:
In the race they call life, do not quit till you're through,
    for the ones who go on earn God's praise.

I've seen people who run with severe handicaps.
    I've seen runners much older than I.
I've felt the respect in the cheers and the claps,
    when someone in a wheel chair rolled by.

The most wonderful thing about running, you see,
    is the fact that you set your own goal.
So no matter how fast or how slow you may be,
    to succeed is within your control.

You may shuffle along, even stagger about,
    in your desperate fight to survive.
But I'd rather do that than give up and get out,
    for a quitter can never arrive.

It's a matter of starting, and doing your best
    to finish each race that you run.
If you stay in the race and trust God for the rest,
    you can say at the end, "I have won!"

LANGUAGE GAMES

I like to play tennis,
even though
I have a lot to learn
about the game.
I'm not going to stop playing
just because
some people don't
understand the game.

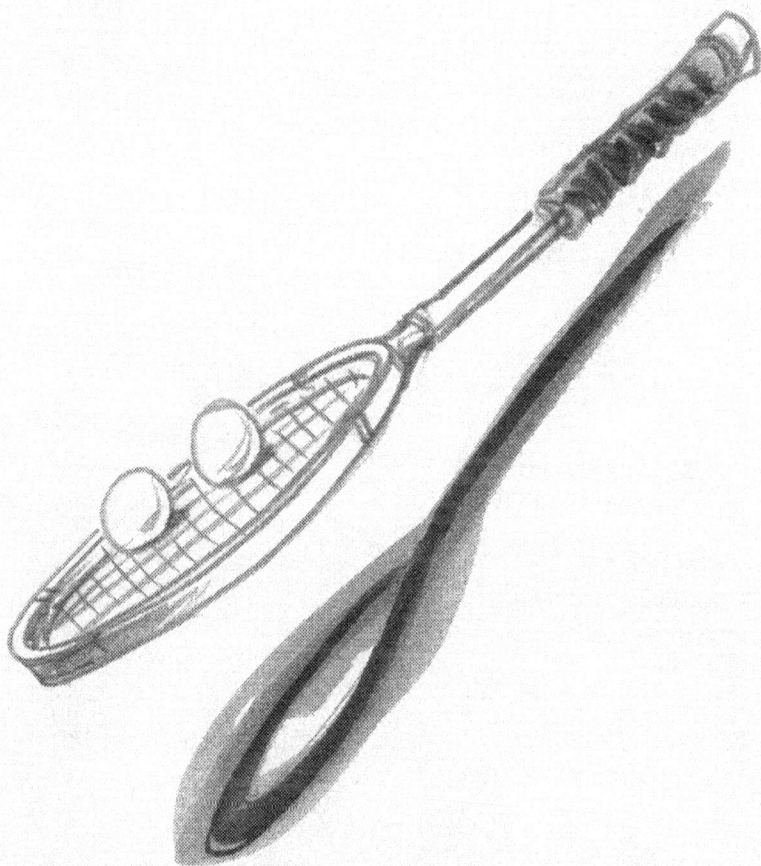

They will never understand it,
unless
they want to learn.
I can help them learn.
Then we can play
and learn
together.
Or at least
we can talk about it,
or maybe watch a game sometime,
together.
I know I can't
make everyone like tennis,
or force it on someone.
Nor can I
impose baseball rules
on tennis games,
or play tennis
on a badminton court,
or make a star
out of someone
with limited potential.
And I know
I can't assume
that someone,
or everyone,
either understands
or wants to play
any game I'm playing,
including tennis.
God talk
is like
tennis.

THREE-TIME LOSERS

For those dolts who believe
that things happen in threes,
isn't this the ridiculous part,
that they cannot conceive,
when they're counting by threes,
it depends on where they choose to start?

CONFESSIONS OF A REFORMED REFORMER

What a burden has been lifted
    from my shoulders ever since
I discovered I'm not gifted
    in my efforts to convince
those I think are awful drivers,
    who should not be on the road,
that they won't be long survivors
    if they fail my drivers' code.
One thing I am not denying:
    I had lost some self-respect,
till at last I gave up trying
    other drivers to correct.
And if I may add one comment,
    things might have become much worse,
had I not learned one bright moment
    I don't run the universe!
And, you know, it is amazing,
    since my views I did revive,
I have found I'm always praising
    how much better people drive!

NEARER MY GOD

In the flying that you do,
has this thought occurred to you:
people are more quick to share,
soaring high up in the air?
Those in an adjacent seat
bare at thirty thousand feet
secrets that they wouldn't tell
even friends they know quite well.
I have also found it true
strangers talk religion, too.
It's as if they find relief,
when they speak of their belief.
Maybe this unconsciously
points to their mortality,
so they talk of faith and God.
That is really not so odd!

BUT HOW MANY DO?

Here's the clue

    to great persuasion:

Have a sense

    of the occasion.

SMOKERS' RIGHTS

Do smokers' rights include the right to jeopardize our health,
    or to ignore the smoking laws of any commonwealth?
Do smokers' rights include the right to foul the air we breathe?
    When people smoke in crowded rooms or offices, I seethe!
Do smokers' rights include the right to throw their butts or stubs
    on office floors or people's lawns, on sidewalks, roads, or
    shrubs?
Do smokers' rights include the right to take offense or grouse
    because non-smokers would prefer they don't smoke in the
    house?
Do smokers want to claim the right to lead their kids astray?
    For kids will smoke tomorrow if their parents smoke today!

WHAT GOES AROUND

You can tell two friends
a secret,
which you caution them
to keep,
but they'll tell four more
and so on,
and a whirlwind
you will reap.
If you want to get
some word out
so that everybody
knows,
tell three people
on the "Q.T."
and you'll see
how fast it goes!
For there always will be
gossips,
and the rumors
will abound.
Just remember that
what goes around
will always
come around.

WHEN THEY'RE SHOOTING AT YOU

What an old embattled "prexy" used to say
    was a logical assumption, in a way:
"If they're shooting at you from the left and right,
    it must mean that you're doing something right."
There's another explanation, I suspect:
    Maybe nothing you are doing is correct!

LADIES AND GENTLEMEN

In the conflict re our language
    there's a point on which I'm shady.
It pertains to the distinction
    'twixt a woman and a lady.
If you call someone the latter,
    all the feminists will bristle,
and no matter what you're saying
    they will quickly blow the whistle.
Now, it may be quite old-fashioned,
    but I think of my own mother
as a lady, yet a woman
    just as free as any other.
And to state it rather bluntly,
    for those folks who are not "fraidies":
Every lady is a woman,
    but all women are not ladies!
That is not a sexist statement,
    for the same is true of men:
While all gentlemen are males, —hey,
    not all males are gentlemen!

THE SNOWMAN

When I pass by
some wintry lawn
and see
a rounded figure
fashioned from the snow,
with button eyes,
a carrot for a nose,
an old felt hat,
a scarf, or tie,
I know
what it would surely say,
if it could speak:
that there is love
within that home,
and joy,
because the silent sentinel
was built
by some excited little girl
or boy
with some parental aid
undoubtedly,
or maybe
by a grown-up
(just for fun),
in whom
a little girl or boy
still lives.
In any case,
I know,
if there is one
upon the lawn,
the people in that house,
if nothing else,

can take the time
to play,
and if there were
more snowmen
on more lawns,
the world would be
a better place
today.

SO DON'T ASK!

To give a "children's sermon"
    is quite a daunting task,
and many pastors stumble
    when they begin to ask
some simple sounding questions,
    their preaching skills to flaunt.
What happens when they don't get
    the answers that they want?
With sometimes shocking candor
    and innocence a child
can make a congregation
    go absolutely wild.
So those who ask a question
    of children must have nerve.
If it's too open-ended,
    they'll get what they deserve!

AFTER DINNER SPEAKER[33]

I was one of several speakers —
some were shriekers, some were squeakers —
representing their professional sports teams.
And because there were so many,
it was not the plan that any
should presume to go on talking to extremes.

On my speech I had been working,
for I don't believe in shirking
a significant responsibility.
I have been of the persuasion
each particular occasion
should determine what one's theme and style should be.

I believed my talk was fitting
for the people who were sitting
for the program in the banquet hall that night,
since it led without confusion
to a powerful conclusion,
which I hoped they all would realize was right.

The main point that I was making
in that verbal undertaking
was not difficult for them to understand.
Yet when I had finished speaking
and the crowd's response was seeking,
I received an unenthusiastic hand.

Now, that same association
in a different location
had another banquet like the one before.
It was only two years later,
and the crowd was even greater —
I would say there were two thousand, maybe more.

By the time that it was my turn
I'd decided not to try earn
their respect by pleading for some noble cause.
So I told three jokes and sat down —
jokes they had not heard in that town —
and I've never had such spirited applause!

The emcee that night, who knew me
from the time before, said to me,
as I sat and gave myself a fat zero,
"It's been two years since I've seen you;
I'm amazed! Really, I mean you
have improved so much since just two years ago!"

What's the moral of this story?
Lessons don't go down in glory,
when an audience would rather be amused.
Just say anything that's funny —
they will eat it up like honey —
And the undiscerning crowd will be enthused.

A PLEA FOR SINGLE TAPS[34]

Some places in Europe have yet to install
    a spigot that blends hot and cold.
Perhaps it's because all their hotels and inns
    are so many hundred years old.

Whenever I see double taps in a sink,
    I know that I'm bound to be burned.
How many the times, while I'm wincing with pain,
    for single-stream faucets I've yearned.

I like to select the right temperature,
    while washing my hands or feet.
The cold is too cold, and the hot is too hot,
    when never the twain shall meet!

NEWS CENTER[35]

My barber is a pundit.
He's up on all the news.
No matter what the topic,
he always has his views.

To get the latest gossip
I know just where to stop.
Forget the local newsstand;
I'll take Joe's barbershop.

MY FAVORITE VERSE

To pick a fav'rite Bible verse is very hard for me —
    so many texts from which to choose, as anyone can see.
And it depends on what the need is on my mind and heart.
    But even then to choose one verse I'd know not where to start.
It's just the same as when I'm asked to name my fav'rite hymn.
    "For what occasion, or which season?" I reply with vim.
"And what's the doctrine or the theme to which it should relate?
    Until I know such things how can my preference I state?"
About my choice there is one thing of which I'm confident:
    The text will be within the Old or the New Testament!

TIME TO STAND

There's another worship custom
that I haven't figured out.
It's as much an iron-clad rule as anything:
Who decided congregations
must stand up on the last line
of the introduction to each hymn they sing?

I once served a congregation
who were always quick to stand,
when they heard the organist begin to play.
It seemed to go much smoother,
and they sang much better, too,
when they all stood up together right away.

YOU CAN'T PLEASE EVERYBODY

Some people tell me I'm too much this way,
    while others tell me I'm too much that way.
It's difficult to know how I can be
    both this and that when those things don't agree.
Some say, "You did too little!" some, "Too much!"
    Some wanted so and so; some, such and such.
The things some people say are downright rude.
    Their caustic comments lead me to conclude:
Some people are impossible to please.
    I dare say you have known a few like these!

Section Three:

FROM MY DISTANT PAST

ODE TO AN ECONOMICS PROFESSOR[36]

Ah, such a soothing voice has he!
They lose themselves in reverie,
as with much pomposity
he builds their curiosity
to the point where they are lost
in a fog. And at whose cost?
Not theirs! But whose, pray tell?
Their dear old Dad's? You ring the bell!
For it is out of Pappy's pocket
that comes the cash. They mock it,
as they slump low in their seats and reap
from his infinite store of knowledge deep
no other benefit than sleep.
For as they dream of days gone by
or promising weekends drawing nigh,
how can they pay him due respect,
when wantonly he does eject
a most insensible line of chatter,
which in the long run doesn't matter?
And as he hems and haws and stutters
and round the speaker's platform putters,
the polysyllabic words he mutters
fall dead on imbecilic ears.
And they through all their college years
must base their many hopes and fears
on just exams. And tears?
Ah, yes, they shall regret,
when instead of tears they sweat
before the angry gaze of him
who judges if they sink or swim.
But if they flunk, they flunk, by Jim!
They won't deny they're in a rut.
Their attitude is just, "So what?"

No sense in suffering like this,
when all the lecture we do miss
because by some decree of Fate
the old boy can't elucidate
to these poor unenlightened souls
his ideal economic goals.
They'd like to cry, "Enough! No more!"
But 'twould be suicide, for sure.
And so they sit there and endure
what seems to them a bitter chore.
And, fearing to disrupt his bliss,
the class is writing —stuff like this!

RETURN TO AN ISLAND[37]

He heeded not the ocean's muffled roar,
 as sweeping waves refreshed the baking sand.
He stood and gazed along the golden shore,
 and brushed his sweating forehead with his hand.

He marveled at the change before his eyes.
 Could such a transformation really be?
Here was indeed an island paradise —
 a tropical oasis of the sea.

The air was still, save for the faintest breeze,
 that breathed upon the greenish tufts a while
and rippled through the bent palmetto trees,
 reluctant to escape this magic isle.

Could this sweet spot that same inferno be,
 where scarce two years before amidst the slain
he prayed to God that he would live to see
 his country, home, and loved ones once again?

No shrieking shells, whose mission to destroy
 leave silhouetted in the blinding glare
 the crumpled, blood-stained body of a boy
 whose eyes, once clear, are fixed in glassy stare.

Not long ago this same enchanted isle
 where now he walked had been a blazing hell.
O demon War, so murderous, so vile,
 because of you now tolls the mourning bell!

Return now to your gloomy heritage
    and rest you from the efforts of your work
of ruin, sorrow, havoc. Let the age
    of peace return anew. You will but lurk

behind the curtain of a few more years,
    till once again you burst upon the world,
when human pride and greed eclipse the tears
    of death, and flags of hatred are unfurled.

God grant the prayer that now bestirs his soul,
    that humankind might learn what ne'er before
their minds have grasped, that this must be the goal:
    to win not wars but peace forever more.

JOOST TO SUDER TO FAIN[38]

Voluminous prose has been written by those
who have this one thought to advance:
that the greatest combine in the double play line
was Tinker to Evers to Chance.

Those three famous Cubs were surely not dubs.
Their fielding was something sublime.
They were far and away the class of their day,
the double play kings of their time.

But they've since been dethroned and partly disowned.
No longer as kings do they reign.
For a new DP team is ruling supreme,
known as Joost to Suder to Fain.

These sensational A's have perfected their ways
to the point where they lead all the rest.
As twin killings go, three years in a row
they've ranked as the major leagues' best.

There's never a worry; they'll comply in a hurry,
when a quick double play is desired.
A roller or liner just couldn't be finer,
you can bet that two men are retired.

You may already know what the record books show,
three years they've continued to shine,
all others surpassing this record amassing:
a total of six twenty-nine!

On second there stands "the man with the hands."
If a ball's hit to Pete there's no doubt.
You never need look, jot it down in the book,
it's a cinch that the batter is out.

Eddie Joost rings the bell as a shortstop as well
as a mighty good man with the stick.
To select someone who has an arm that's as true,
it would be an impossible pick.

A hitter's accursed with Ferris on first.
There's no one as clever as he,
in spearing a bounder or sizzling grounder
and completing that tough three-six-three.

A long time from now, when they're telling of how
so and so could get two with no strain,
we'll think of the days of Connie Mack's A's,
and of Joost and Suder and Fain.

NOTES

1. Philippians 2:3 - Do nothing from selfishness or conceit, but in humility count others better than yourselves.
2. Matthew 22:14 - "For many are called, but few are chosen."
3. John 6:66-67 - After this many of his disciples drew back and no longer went about with him. 67 Jesus said to the twelve, "Will you also go away?"
4. Psalm 118:24 - This is the day which the LORD has made; let us rejoice and be glad in it.
5. Matthew 2:10-11 - When they saw the star, they rejoiced exceedingly with great joy; 11 and going into the house they saw the child with Mary his mother, and they fell down and worshiped him. . .
6. 1 John 3:18 - Little children, let us not love in word or speech but in deed and in truth.
7. Proverbs 16:18 - Pride goes before destruction, and a haughty spirit before a fall.
8. Proverbs 26:18-19 - Like a maniac who shoots deadly firebrands and arrows, 19 so is one who deceives a neighbor and says, "I am only joking!" (NRSV)
9. Luke 11:43 - "Woe to you Pharisees! for you love the best seat in the synagogues and salutations in the market places."
10. Matthew 17:24-27 - ". . . Go to the sea and cast a hook, and take the first fish that comes up, and when you open its mouth you will find a shekel; take that and give it to them for me and for yourself."
11. I Corinthians 4:19-20 - "But I will come to you soon, if the Lord wills, and I will find out not the talk of these arrogant people but their power. 20 For the kingdom of God does not consist in talk but in power."
12. 1 Corinthians 9:19-22 - For though I am free with respect to all, I have made myself a slave to all, so that I might win more of them. 20 To the Jews I became as a Jew, in order to win Jews. To those under the law I became as one under the

law (though I myself am not under the law) so that I might win those under the law. 21 To those outside the law I became as one outside the law (though I am not free from God's law but am under Christ's law) so that I might win those outside the law. 22 To the weak I became weak, so that I might win the weak. I have become all things to all people, that I might by all means save some. (NRSV)

13. Matthew 6:19-20 - "Do not lay up for yourselves treasures on earth, where moth and rust consume and where thieves break in and steal, 20 but lay up for yourselves treasures in heaven, where neither moth nor rust consumes and where thieves do not break in and steal."

14. Matthew 19:13-15 - Then children were brought to him that he might lay his hands on them and pray. The disciples rebuked the people; 14 but Jesus said, "Let the children come to me, and do not hinder them; for to such belongs the kingdom of heaven." 15 And he laid his hands on them and went away.

15. Matthew 16:23 - But he turned and said to Peter, "Get behind me, Satan! You are a stumbling block to me; for you are setting your mind not on divine things but on human things." (NRSV)

16. Matthew 21:28-31a - "What do you think? A man had two sons; and he went to the first and said, 'Son, go and work in the vineyard today.' 29 And he answered, 'I will not'; but afterward he repented and went. 30 And he went to the second and said the same; and he answered, 'I go, sir,' but did not go. 31 Which of the two did the will of his father?"

17. Isaiah 24:5 - The earth lies polluted under its inhabitants; for they have transgressed laws, violated the statutes, broken the everlasting covenant. (NRSV)

18. Isaiah 30:1-5 - Oh, rebellious children, says the LORD, who carry out a plan, but not mine; who make an alliance, but against my will, adding sin to sin; 2 who set out to go down to Egypt without asking for my counsel, to take refuge in the protection of Pharaoh, and to seek shelter in the shadow of Egypt; 3 Therefore the protection of Pharaoh shall become your shame, and the shelter in the shadow of Egypt your

humiliation. 4 For though his officials are at Zoan and his envoys reach Hanes, 5 everyone comes to shame through a people that cannot profit them, that brings neither help nor profit, but shame and disgrace. (NRSV)

19. Acts 8:35 - Then Philip opened his mouth, and beginning with this scripture he told him the good news of Jesus.

20. Mark 1:35 - Very early in the morning, while it was still dark, Jesus got up. . . (NIV)

21. Mark 1:35 - Very early in the morning, while it was still dark, Jesus got up, left the house, and went off to a solitary place, where he prayed. (NIV)

22. I Corinthians 1:23 - But we preach Christ crucified, a stumbling block to Jews and folly to Gentiles. . .

23. Acts 18:27b - . . . When (Paul) arrived, he greatly helped those who through grace had believed.

24. Isaiah 49:7-18 - Thus says the LORD, the Redeemer of Israel and his Holy One, to one deeply despised, abhorred by the nations, the slave of rulers, "Kings shall see and stand up, princes, and they shall prostrate themselves, because of the LORD, who is faithful, the Holy One of Israel, who has chosen you." . . . (NRSV)

25. Genesis 7:2 - Take with you seven pairs of all clean animals, the male and his mate; and a pair of the animals that are not clean, the male and his mate.

26. Luke 7:36-39 - One of the Pharisees asked him to eat with him, and he went into the Pharisee's house, and took his place at table. 37 And behold, a woman of the city, who was a sinner, when she learned that he was at table in the Pharisee's house, brought an alabaster flask of ointment, 38 and standing behind him at his feet, weeping, she began to wet his feet with her tears, and wiped them with the hair of her head, and kissed his feet, and anointed them with the ointment. 39 Now when the Pharisee who had invited him saw it, he said to himself, "If this man were a prophet, he would have known who and what sort of woman this is who is touching him, for she is a sinner."

27. Luke 11:15 - But some of them said, "He casts out demons by Beelzebul, the ruler of the demons." (NRSV)
28. Luke 2:48 - When his parents saw him they were astonished; and his mother said to him, "Child, why have you treated us like this? Look, your father and I have been searching for you in great anxiety." (NRSV)
29. Romans 2:1 - Therefore you have no excuse, whoever you are, when you judge others; for in passing judgment on another you condemn yourself, because you, the judge, are doing the very same things. (NRSV)
30. Romans 12:2 - Do not be conformed to this world. . .
31. Romans 14:5 - Some judge one day to be better than another, while others judge all days to be alike. Let all be fully convinced in their own minds. (NRSV)
32. Romans 12:19 - Beloved, never avenge yourselves, but leave it to the wrath of God; for it is written, "Vengeance is mine, I will repay, says the Lord."
33. This poem describes two related incidents which occurred during my tenure with the Philadelphia Athletics. They taught me a lesson I'll never forget.
34. This commentary on European wash basin fixtures was written years ago, after a conversation with a fellow traveler who had had as much difficulty with the separate spigots as I had.
35. I have been going to the same barber for many years. Joe Guido and his gregarious colleagues are an effective news agency!
36. This is the oldest poem in this volume. The bulk of it was written during what to me was a most boring lecture by an economics professor, in whose mid-afternoon class I wasn't the only student who had trouble staying awake. I was a not too highly motivated, 19-year-old college sophomore at the time, soon to begin active duty in the Navy in World War II.
37. This poem was written in August, 1945, while I was serving aboard the U.S.S. Chandeleur (AV10). Having recently visited the island after it had been recaptured by the American forces, I was reflecting on what it might have been like for a soldier

to return to the scene of the bloody conflict in which he had participated two years earlier.

38. There may still be a few baseball fans, like my friend Lyle Schaller, who remember Connie Mack and his Philadelphia Athletics, winners of eight American League pennants and five World Series. A few may even remember the stellar infield combination of Eddie Joost, Peter Suder, and Ferris Fain, who established an impressive double play record during their heyday. Their exploits were celebrated in this poem, which was sent out as a press release and appeared in newspapers throughout the baseball playing world. I was public relations and publicity director of the Athletics at the time. The poem is included here for people like Lyle.

Index of First Lines

Topical Index

www.ingramcontent.com/pod-product-compliance
Lightning Source LLC
Chambersburg PA
CBHW071638050426
42443CB00026B/728